Pipe-Major W. ROSS'S COLLECTION

OF

HIGHLAND BAGPIPE MUSIC

BOOK 4

All tunes in this Book are arranged by
Pipe-Major W. Ross and are copyright.

PATERSON'S PUBLICATIONS

CONTENTS BOOK IV

The Burning of the Piper's Hut

March

Royal Scottish Pipers Society

March

R. Campbell

Cairo to Tunis

March

Piper A. Williams
Ist. Battn. Gordon Highlanders

The Highland Division at Akarit

March

Piper W. McDonald
5th. Battn. Seaforth Highlanders

Mrs Margaret Anderson of Craigellachie

March

Angus MacPherson

Maclean of Pennycross

March

Pipe Major A. Ferguson

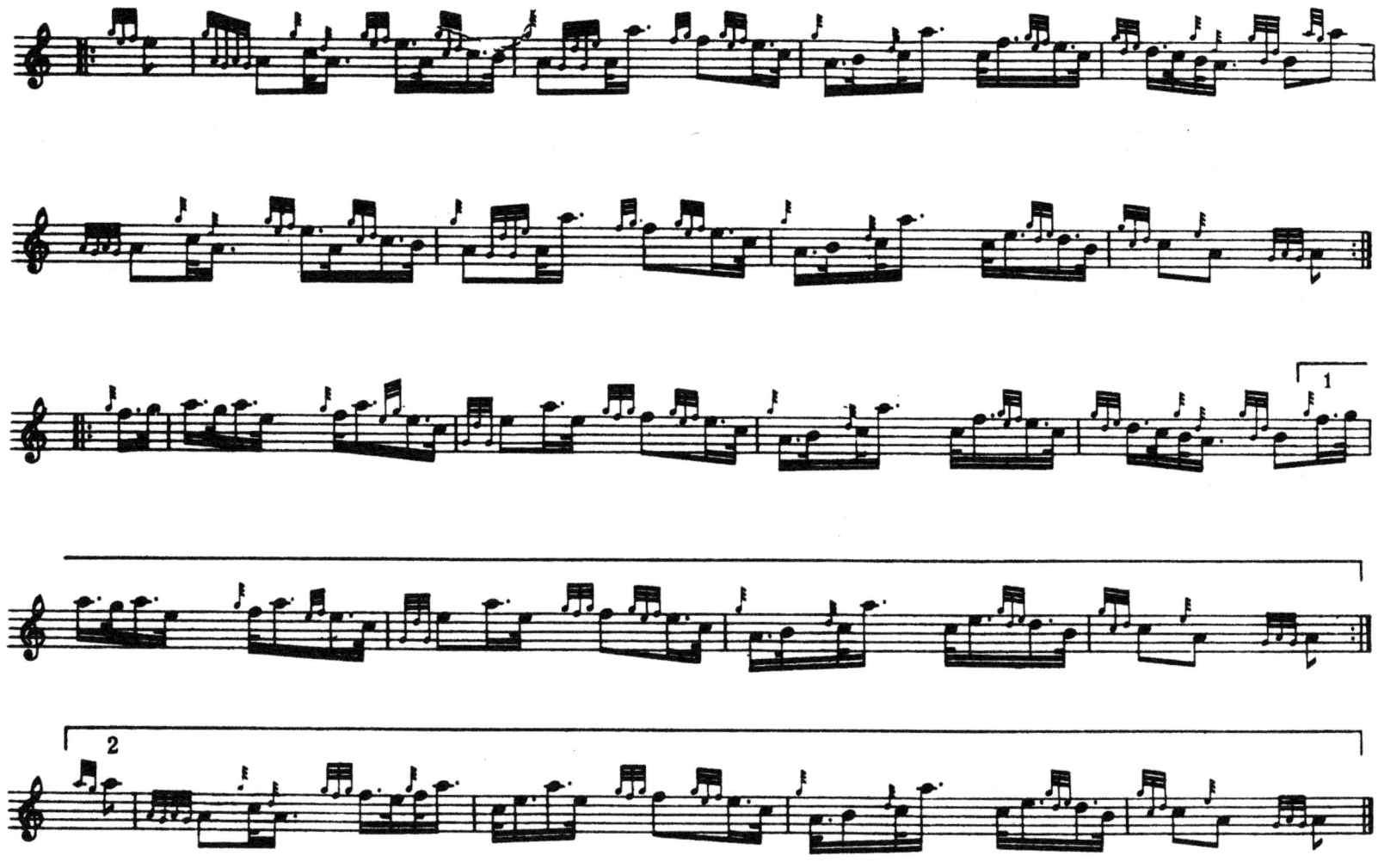

The Relief of Ladysmith

March

Major K. M. Cameron, R. A. M. C.

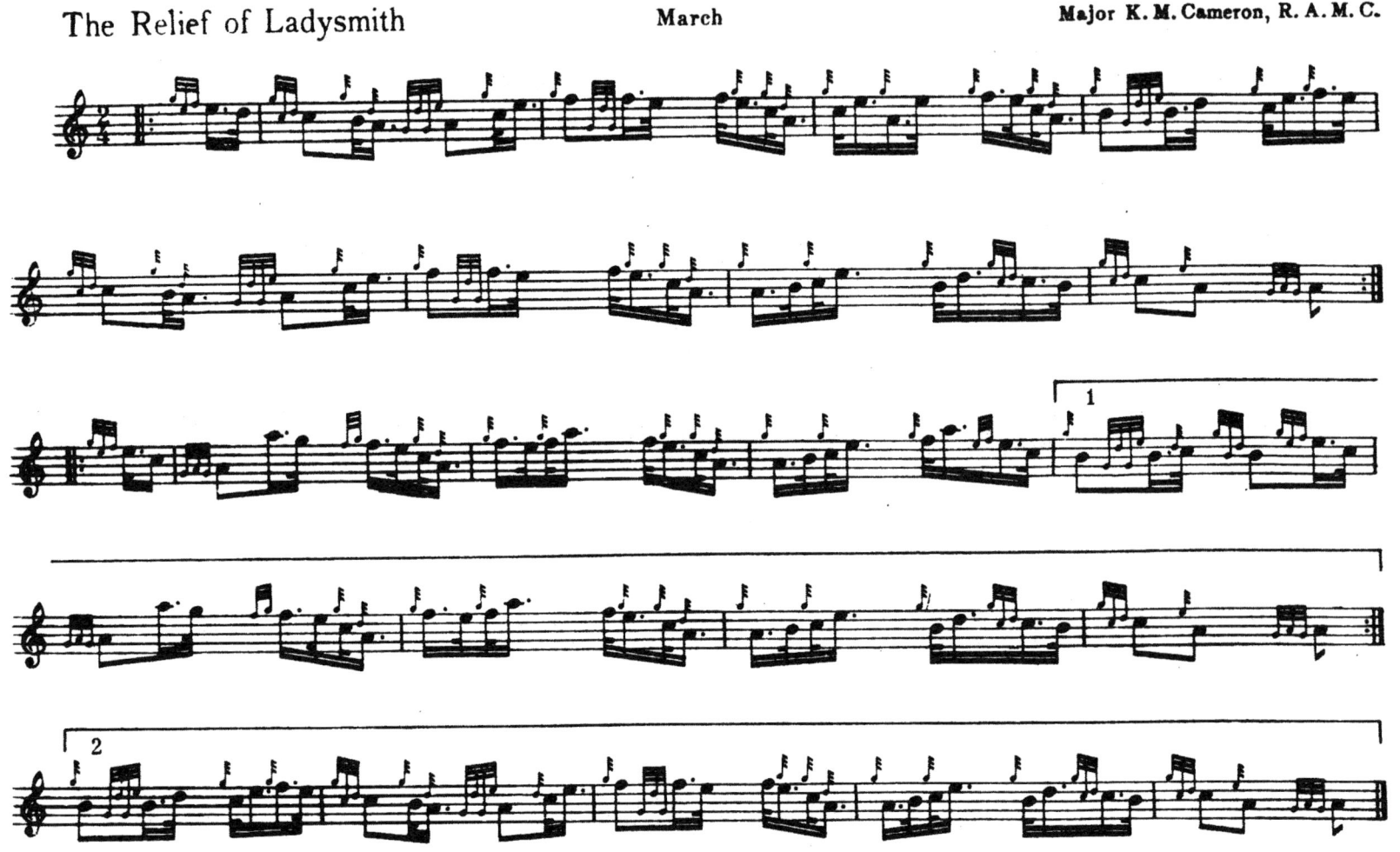

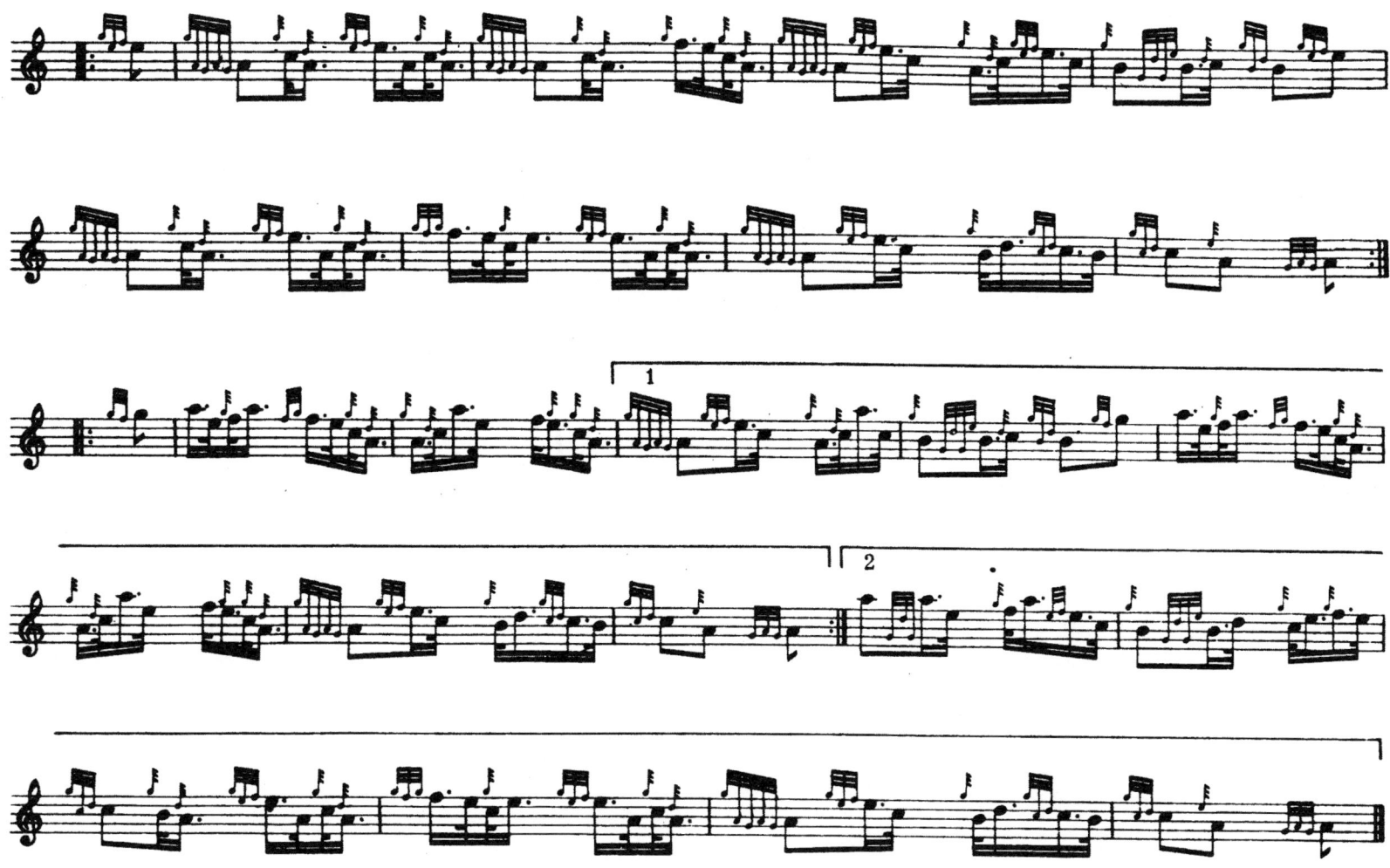

J. Douglas Ramsay Esq., of Bamff

March

P. M. Meldrum

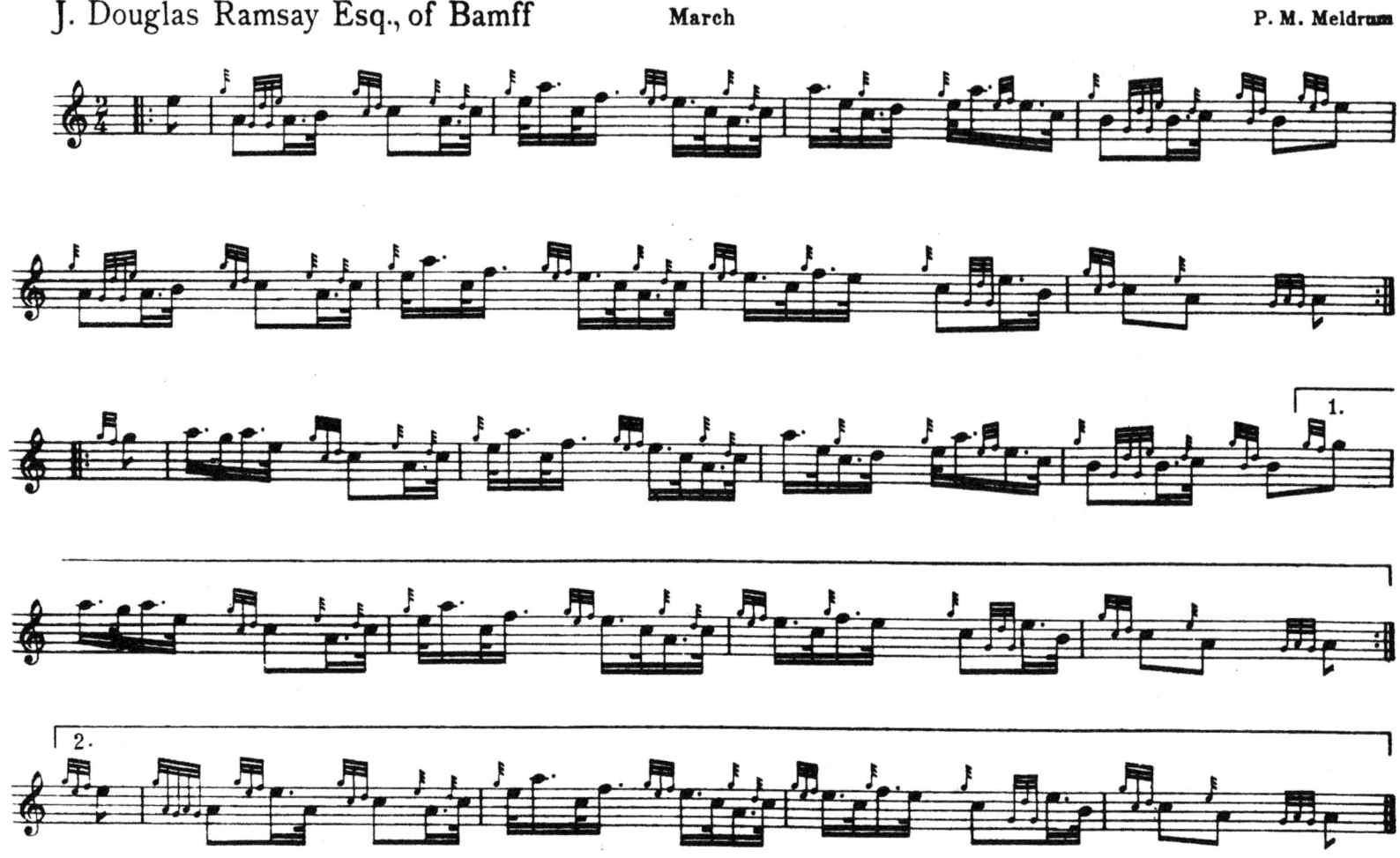

The Marchioness of Tullibardine

March

A. Duff

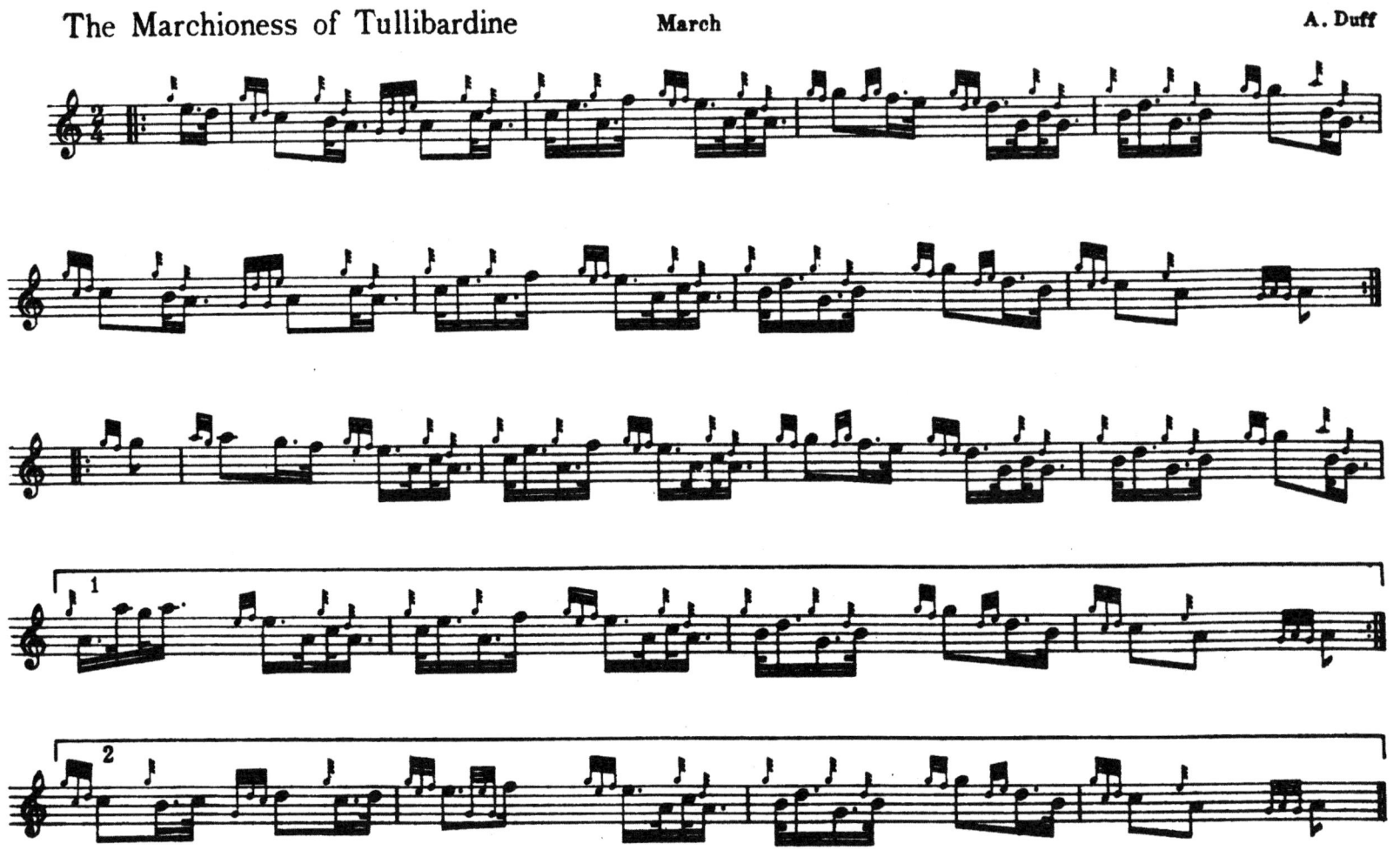

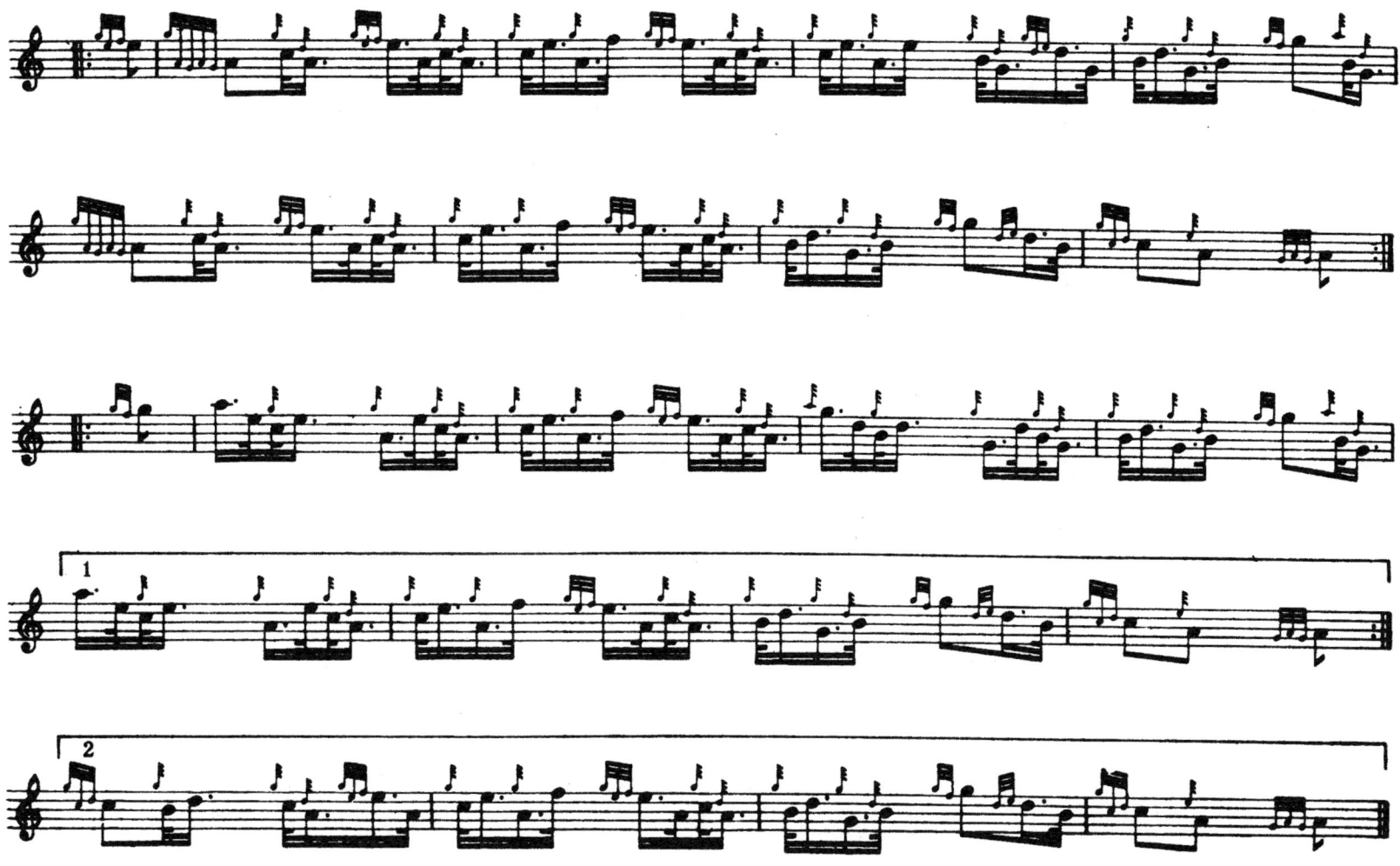

The Conundrum

March

P. R. Macleod

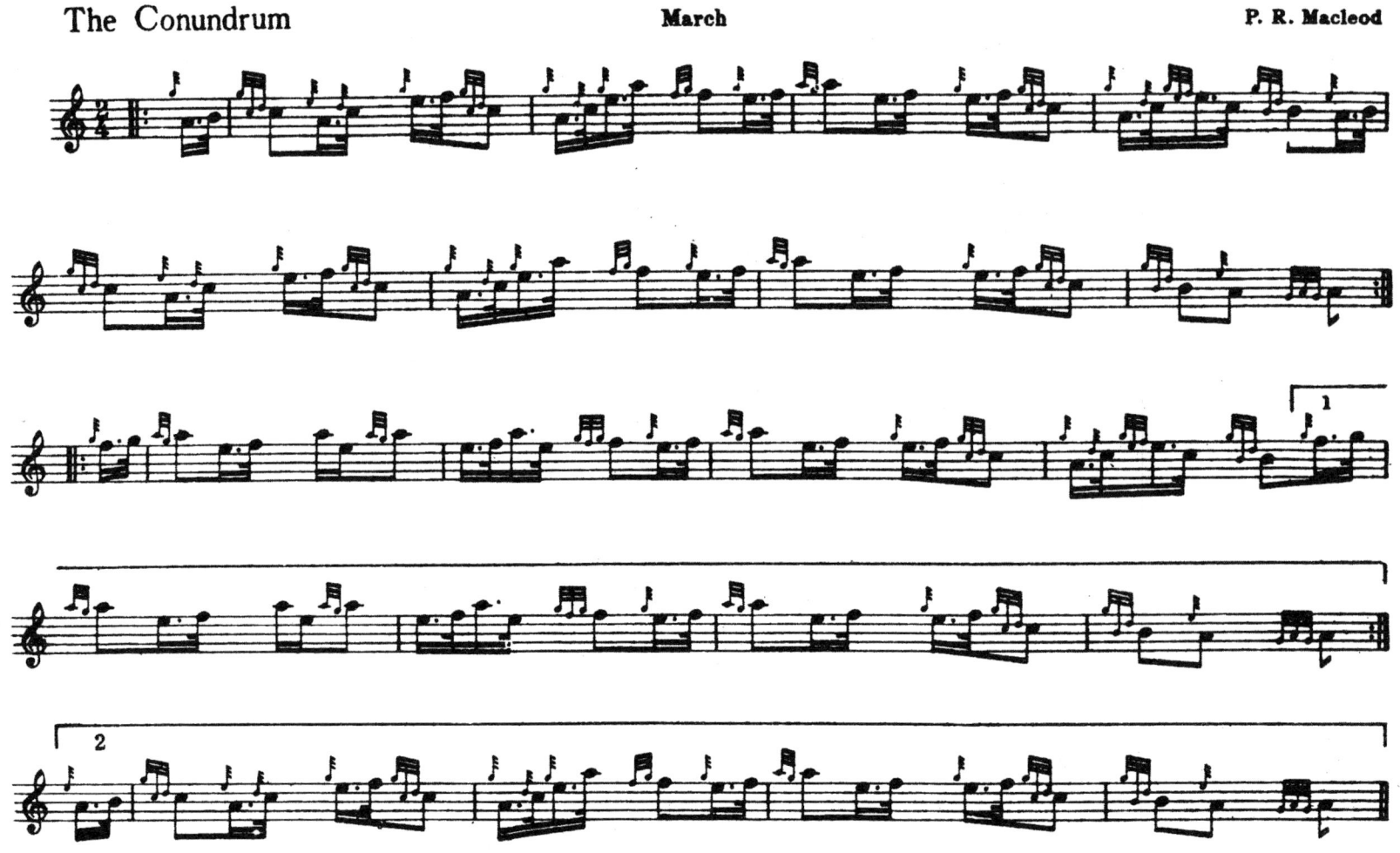

Millbank Cottage

March

W. D. Dumbreck

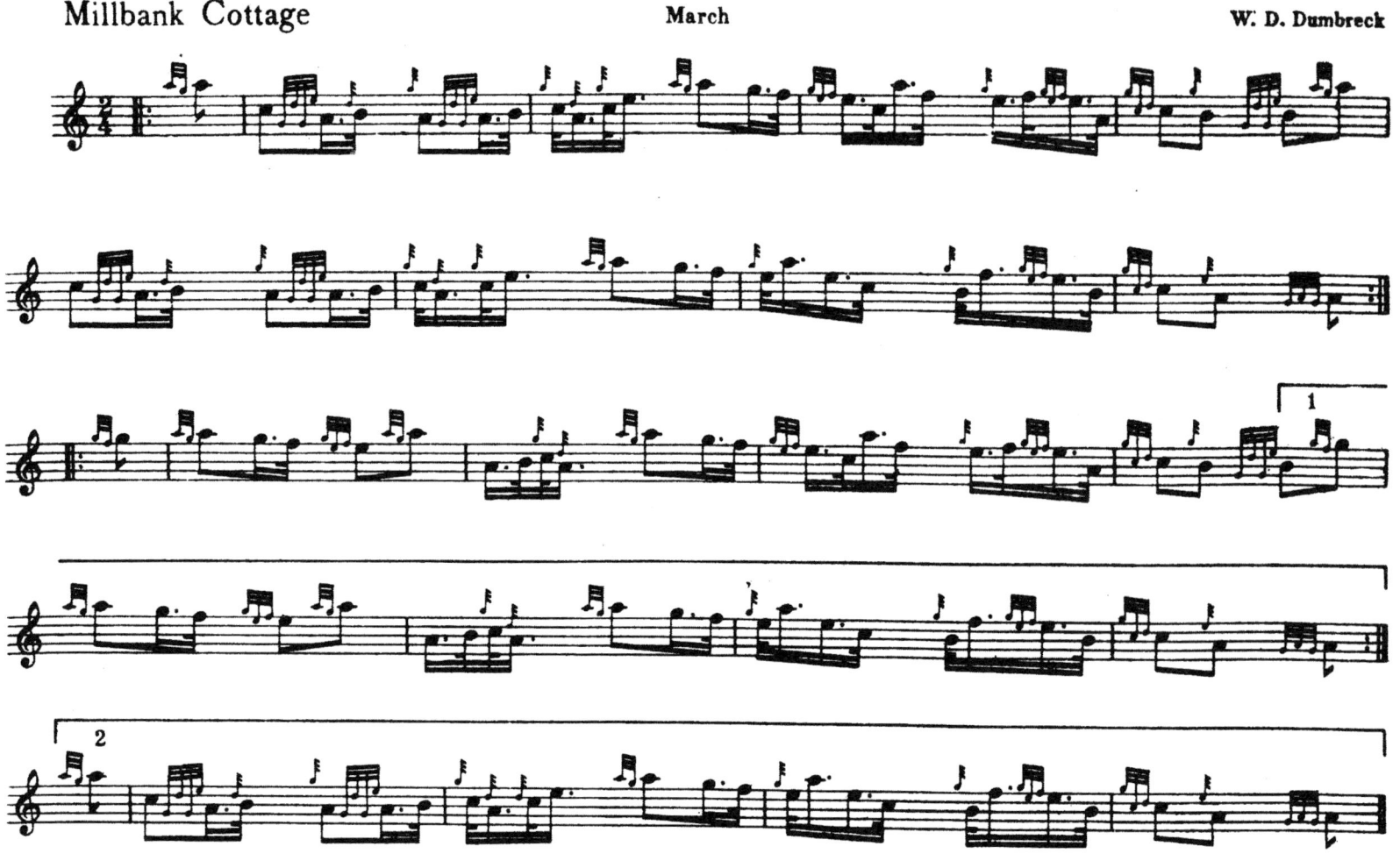

Angus MacPherson of Inveran

March

W. MacDonald
Gruid

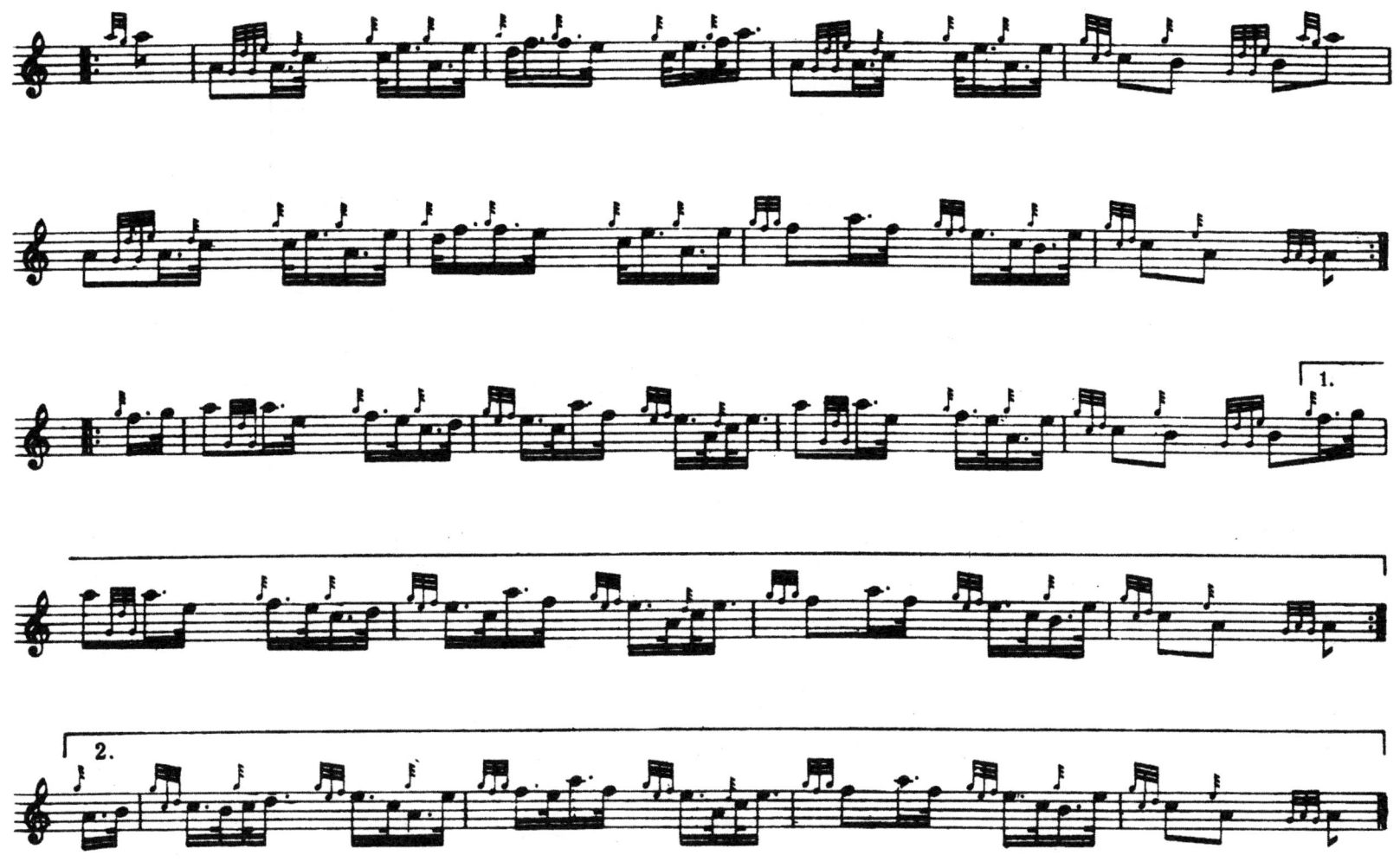

The Balmoral Highlanders

March

Angus MacKay

The Braes of Brecklet

March

W. Lawrie

The 74th's Farewell to Edinburgh

March

W. MacKinnon

Arthur Bignold of Lochrosque

March

John MacColl

The 93rd's Farewell to Parkhurst

March

P. M. R. Meldrum

The 78th Regiment

March

1848

Archibald Campbell of Kilberry

Slow March

John MacColl

The Glasgow Caithness Centenary Gathering

Slow March

P. M. W. M. Taylor

The 75th's Entry to Tripoli

March

Piper Williams

2nd time of 2nd Part

1st time

2nd time of 4th Part

1st time

The 51st Highland Division

March

Pipe Major D. Macleod.

Aberlour House

Strathspey

The Dounie Weaver

Strathspey

The Dunkeld Highlanders

March

Duncan Campbell
1848

Nellie's Strathspey

Roderick MacDonald

Strathspey

Mrs MacDonald of Dunach

Strathspey

John MacColl

Balmoral Castle

Strathspey

A. MacKay

Dorrotor Bridge

Strathspey

J. Braidwood

The Fourth of June

Strathspey

J. Graham Campbell

Lady Loudon

Strathspey

The Merry Maids of Sunnyside

Reel

R. Ireland

The Grey Bob

Reel

Scorrybreck Falls

Reel

P. M. P. Bain

Duntroon

Reel

Colonel MacLeod

Reel

The Wren's Death

Reel

Bristly Beard

Reel

44 Kenny would dance with the maid

Paddy's Leather Breeches

Auntie Cairistion

Jig

Iain MacPherson

Minnie Hynd

Jig

P. M. D. MacLean

Mike Cassidy

Jig

Cuairt Nam Fir-eun Og (The Flight of the Eaglets) (MacRoberts Lament) Slow Air

W. Ross

Loch Monar

Slow Air

W. Ross

The Heroes of Dunkirk

Retreat

P. M. D. MacLeod

THE COUNTESS OF DYSARTS WELCOME TO EDINBURGH CASTLE   Retreat   W. Ross